Musical Storyland

A SING-ALONG BOOK with Musical Disc

Words and Music by
DAVID BOWIE

Illustrations by
JAMILLA NAJI

Worlds In Ink Publishing
San Diego, California

Published in the United States by Worlds In Ink Publishing, San Diego, CA.
www.WorldsInInk.com

For sale exclusively in the United States of America

The illustrations for this book were rendered in acrylic on canvas.

Book designed by Christopher Bryson
www.WaxedPaperPress.com

ISBN 0-9745568-0-7

Library of Congress control number: 2003097082

Printed in Hong Kong

This book is dedicated to David Bowie whose music has made my world a much happier place.

TABLE OF CONTENTS

 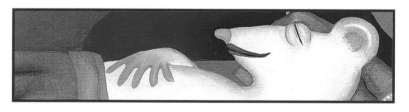

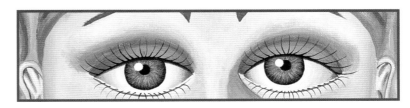

LET'S START SINGING!

IT'S MUSIc WE'RE BRINGING!

UNCLE ARTHUR

Strikes the bell for five o'clock
Uncle Arthur closes shop
Screws the tops on all the bottles
Turns the lights out, locks it up

Climbs across his bike and he's away
Cycles past the gas works, past the river
Down the high street, back to mother
It's another empty day

Uncle Arthur likes his mummy
Uncle Arthur still reads comics
Uncle Arthur follows Batman

Round and round the rumors fly
How he ran away from mum
On his thirty-second birthday
Told her that he'd found a chum

Mother cried and raved and yelled and fussed
Arthur left her no illusion
Brought the girl round, saved confusion
Sally was the real thing, not just lust
Uncle Arthur vanished quickly
Uncle Arthur and his new bride
Uncle Arthur follows Sally

Round and round goes Arthur's head
Hasn't eaten well for days
Little Sally may be lovely
But cooking leaves her in a maze

Uncle Arthur packed his bags and fled
Back to mother, all's forgiven
Serving in the fam'ly shop
He gets his pocket money. He's well fed

Uncle Arthur passed the gas works
Uncle Arthur passed the river
Uncle Arthur down the high street
Uncle Arthur follows mother

RUBBER BAND

Rubber Band
There's a rubber band that plays tunes out of tune
In the library garden Sunday afternoon
While a little chappie waves a golden wand

Rubber Band
In 1912 I was so handsome and so strong
My mustache was stiffly waxed and one foot long
And I loved a girl while you played teatime tunes

Dear Rubber Band, you're playing my tune out of tune

Rubber Band
Won't you play your haunting theme again for me
While I eat my scones and drink my cup of tea
The sun is warm, but it's a lonely afternoon

Oh play that tune

Rubber Band
How I wish that I had joined your Rubber Band
We'd have played in lively parks throughout the land
And one Sunday afternoon, I'd find my love

Rubber Band
In the '14-'18 war I went to sea
Thought my Sunday love was waiting home for me
Now she's married to the leader of your band

THERE IS A HAPPY LAND

There is a happy land where only children live
They don't have the time to learn the ways of you sir
Mister Grown-up

There's a special place in the rhubarb fields underneath the leaves
It's a secret place and adults aren't allowed there, Mister Grown-up
Go away, sir

Charlie Brown's got half a crown, he's goin' to buy a kite
Jimmy's ill with chicken pox and Tommy's learnt to ride his bike
Tiny Tim sings prayers and hymns, he's so small we don't notice him
He gets in the way but we always let him play with us

Mother calls but we don't hear, there's lots more things to do
It's only five o-clock and we're not tired yet
But we will be very shortly

Sissy Steven plays with girls, someone made him cry
Tony climbed a tree and fell, trying hard to touch the sky
Tommy lit a fire one day, nearly burnt the fields away
Tommy's mom found out, but he put the blame on me and Ray

There is a happy land where only children live
You've had your chance and now the doors are closed sir, Mister Grown-up
Go away, sir

Do do do do do do do do do do do do do do do do do do

DID YOU EVER HAVE A DREAM?

Did you ever have a dream or two
Where the hero is a guy named you?
And the things he does are just too much

Does he fly like Mister Superman
Speak Chinese, French and Dutch?
Did you ever have a dream or two?

Have you ever woken up one day
With the feeling that you've been away?
If the girl that you dreamed of last night
Had the very same dream
In the very same scene
With the very same boy, hold tight!

It's a very special knowledge that you've got
My friend
You can travel anywhere with any one you care
It's a very special knowledge that you've got
My friend
You can walk around in New York
While you sleep in Penge

I will travel round the world one night
On the magic wings of astral flight
If you've got the secret, tell me do
Have you ever had a dream or two?

It's a very special knowledge that you've got
My friend
You can travel anywhere with any one you care
It's a very special knowledge that you've got
My friend
You can walk around in New York
While you sleep in Penge

I will travel round the world one night
On the magic wings of astral flight
If you've got the secret, tell me do

Have you ever had a dream or two?
Have you ever had a dream or two?

SELL ME A COAT

A winter's day, a bitter snowflake on my face
My summer girl takes little backward steps away
Jack Frost took her hand and left me
Jack Frost ain't so cool

Sell me a coat with buttons of silver
Sell me a coat that's red or gold
Sell me a coat with little patch pockets
Sell me a coat 'cause I feel cold

And when she smiles, the ice forgets to melt away
Not like before
Her smile was warm in yesterday
See the trees like silver candy, feel my icy hands

Sell me a coat with buttons of silver
Sell me a coat that's red or gold
Sell me a coat with little patch pockets
Sell me a coat 'cause I feel cold

See my eyes, my window pane
See my tears like gentle rain
That's the memory of a summer day

Sell me a coat with buttons of silver
Sell me a coat that's red or gold
Sell me a coat with little patch pockets
Sell me a coat 'cause I feel cold

COME AND BUY MY TOYS

Smiling girls and rosy boys, come and buy my little toys
Monkeys made of gingerbread and sugar horses painted red
Rich men's children running past their fathers dressed in hose
Golden hair and mud of many acres on their shoes
Gazing eyes and running wild, past the stocks and over stiles
Kiss the wind o merry child, but come and buy my toys

You've watched your father plough the fields with a ram's horn
Sowed it wide with peppercorn and furrowed with a bramble thorn
Reaped it with a sharpened scythe, threshed it with a quill
The miller told your father that he'd work it with the greatest will

Now your watching's over, you must play with girls and boys
Leave the parsley on the stalls, come and buy my toys
You shall own a cambric shirt
You shall work your father's land
But now you shall play in the market square
Till you be a man

Smiling girls and rosy boys
Come and buy my little toys
Monkeys made of ginger bread
And sugar horses painted red

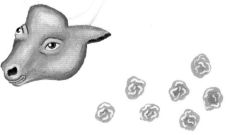

MAID OF BOND STREET

This girl is made of lipstick
Powder and paint
Sees the pictures of herself
Every magazine on every shelf

This girl is maid of Bond Street
Hailing cabs, lunches with executives
Gleaming teeth sip aperitifs

This girl is a lonely girl
Takes the train from Paddington to Oxford Circus
Buys the Daily News
But passengers don't smile at her
Oh no, don't smile at her

This girl is made of loneliness
A broken heart
For the boy that she once knew
Doesn't want to know her any more

And this girl is a lonely girl
Everything she wants is hers
But she can't make it with the boy
She really wants to be with
All the time, to love, all the time

This boy is made of envy
Jealousy
He doesn't have a limousine
Really wants to be a star himself
This girl, her world is made of flashlights and films
Her cares are scraps on the cutting room floor

And maids of Bond Street
Drive round in chauffered cars
Maids of Bond Street picture clothes, eyes of stars
Maids of Bond Street shouldn't have worldly cares
Maids of Bond Street shouldn't have love affairs

LOVE YOU TILL TUESDAY

Just look through your window, look who sits outside
Little me is waiting, standing through the night
When you walk out through your door
I'll wave my flag and shout

Ah beautiful baby
My burning desire started on Sunday
Give me your heart and I'll love you till Tuesday

Da da da dum
Da da da dum

Who's that hiding in the apple tree
Clinging to a branch?
Don't be afraid, it's only me
Hoping for a little romance
If you lie beneath my shade
I'll keep you nice and cool

Ah beautiful baby
I was very lonely till I met you on Sunday
My passion's never ending and I'll love you till Tuesday

Da da da dum, Da da da dum
Da da da dum, Da da da dum
Let the wind blow through your hair
Be nice to the big blue sea

Don't be afraid of the man in the moon
Because it's only me
I shall always want you
Until my love runs dry

Ah beautiful baby
My heart's a-flame
I'll love you till Tuesday
My head's in a whirl
And I'll love you till Tuesday
Love, love, love, love, love you till Tuesday
Love, love, love, love, love you till Tuesday

Da da da dum, Da da da dum
Da da da dum, Da da da dum
Da da da dum, Da da da dum
Da da da dum, Da da da dum

Well, I might be able to stretch it till Wednesday

WHEN I LIVE MY DREAM

When I live my dream I'll take you with me
Riding on a golden horse
We'll live within my castle with people there to serve you
Happy at the sound of your voice

Maybe I'll slay a dragon for you
Or banish wicked giants from the land
But you will find that nothing in my dream can hurt you
We will only love each other
As forever when I live my dream

When I live my dream I'll forgive the things you told me
And the empty man you left behind
It's a broken heart that dreams, it's a broken heart you left me
Only love can live in my dreams

I'll wish and the thunder clouds will vanish
Wish and the storm will fade away
Wish again and you will stand before me
While the sky will paint an overture
And trees will play the rhythm of my dream

When I live my dream, please be there to meet me
Let me be the one to understand
When I live my dream, I'll forget the hurt you gave me
Then we can live in our new land

Till the day my dream cascades around me
I'm content to let you pass me by
Till that day you'll run to many other men
But let them know it's just for now
Tell them that I've got a dream and tell them
You're the starring role
Tell them I'm a dreaming kind of guy
And I'm gonna make my dream
Tell them I will live my dream
Tell them they can laugh at me
But don't forget your date with me
When I live my dream

CHING-A-LING

While flying through an azure cloud
A crystal girl I spied
She kissed the blue-bird's honey tongue
who stuttered as she sighed:

"I wish to sing the Ching-ling song
The Ching-ling song is fine
I'd give my jewels and caviar
To make this day-dream mine"

Ching-A-Ling, Ching-A-Ling, Ching-A-Ling
Ching-A-Ling, Ching-A-Ling, Ching-A-Ling
Ching-A-Ling, Ching-A-Ling, Ching-A-Ling
Ching-A-Ling, Ching-A-Ling

While stepping through a heaven's eye
Two lover souls we spied
Their wispy cloud voice sang to me
A tearful happy cry

"We love to play our love strung harps
No fetters do we know
No gifts of money do we give
For love is all we own"

Na na na na na na na na na na na na na na

How This Book Came To Be

The foundations for this book were established in 1973, when I was eleven years old. In my big brother's bedroom, I found an eight-track tape titled Images, which had been written and recorded by David Bowie during the period between 1966 and 1970. I slipped the tape into my brother's stereo and was instantly spellbound. After receiving my own stereo as a present for my twelfth birthday, I purchased the two-record vinyl version of Images for myself. I listened and I listened, again and again. The characters described in the music were so colorful and curious that I daydreamed about them through the remainder of my childhood. As I continued to listen to the music, more and more details of the fabulous characters and scenes began to form in my imagination. My first painting efforts involved my own interpretations of songs included on this delightful recording.

As an adult my passion for David Bowie's early recordings grew stronger. In my late thirties when I became pregnant, I pictured my little girl singing and dancing to my favorite tunes. It was then that I decided to transform my lifelong dream into a tangible reality. My goal was to record a selection of favorite songs on disc, then include them in a book with written lyrics and colorful illustrations. My hope was that this format would help children navigate the transition from the spoken word to the written word, while exposing them to music and visual art.

This book is the result of what has been both an enjoyable and demanding exploration. With much encouragement from family and friends, I am now able to share my years of daydreams with you. My hope is that the words, music and pictures in this book serve to enrich your imagination and live with you for a lifetime.

www.MusicalStoryland.com

CREDITS FOR LYRICS USED IN THIS BOOK

CREDITS FOR MUSICAL DISC

UNCLE ARTHUR
Artist: David Bowie
Writer: David Bowie
©TRO–Essex Music, Inc.
℗ 1967 Decca Music Group Limited

COME AND BUY MY TOYS
Artist: David Bowie
Writer: David Bowie
©TRO–Essex Music, Inc.
℗ 1967 Decca Music Group Limited

RUBBER BAND
(1966 version)
Artist: David Bowie
Writer: David Bowie
©EMI Al Gallico Music Corp.
℗ 1966 Decca Music Group Limited

MAID OF BOND STREET
Artist: David Bowie
Writer: David Bowie
©Embassy Music Corporation.
℗ 1967 Decca Music Group Limited

THERE IS A HAPPY LAND
Artist: David Bowie
Writer: David Bowie
©TRO–Essex Music, Inc.
℗ 1967 Decca Music Group Limited

LOVE YOU TILL TUESDAY
Artist: David Bowie
Writer: David Bowie
©TRO–Essex Music, Inc.
℗ 1967 Decca Music Group Limited

DID YOU EVER HAVE A DREAM
Artist: David Bowie
Writer: David Bowie
©TRO–Essex Music, Inc.
℗ 1967 Decca Music Group Limited

WHEN I LIVE MY DREAM
Artist: David Bowie
Writer: David Bowie
©TRO–Essex Music, Inc.
℗ 1967 Decca Music Group Limited

SELL ME A COAT
(1967 version)
Artist: David Bowie
Writer: David Bowie
©TRO–Essex Music, Inc.
℗ 1967 Decca Music Group Limited

CHING-A-LING
(1984 version)
Artist: David Bowie
Writer: David Bowie
©TRO–Essex Music, Inc.
℗ 1967 Decca Music Group Limited

TECHNICHAL CREDITS

All artwork photographed by Charles Thorsten
Carol Landry Photography
San Diego, CA
Carollandry@sbcglobal.net
www.PhotosOverTheNet.com

Title Page Illustration
"Miracles Happen" 21" x 12"
Acrylic on Brass
By Jamilla Naji
From the collection of Michael S. Berg
Used by permission

Editorial Consultant, Cynthia L. Swope

Book Layout and Jacket Design by Christopher Bryson
www.WaxedPaperPress.com